Letter To The Shooter

Poetry About Thomas Matthew Crooks

by JMR

978-1-300-74047-6
Imprint: Lulu.com
Trade Paperback.
*Letter To The Shooter: Poetry About
Thomas Matthew Crooks*
By JMR

Introduction

On July 13th, 2024, the news rang out around the country that former president Donald Trump survived an assassination attempt. Then came the conspiracy theories that flew around the Internet and, especially social media, which were mixed with hatred against the shooter... because he missed. So many people – too many people – were just breaking Federal Law 18 U.S. Code § 871: *"Whoever knowingly and willfully deposits for conveyance in the mail or for a delivery from any post office or by any letter carrier any letter, paper, writing, print, missive, or document containing any threat to take the life of, to kidnap, or to inflict bodily harm upon the President of the United*

States, the President-elect, the Vice President or other officer next in the order of succession to the office of President of the United States, or the Vice President-elect, or knowingly and willfully otherwise makes any such threat against the President, President-elect, Vice President or other officer next in the order of succession to the office of President, or Vice President-elect, shall be fined under this title or imprisoned not more than five years, or both." The Internet was full of memes, postings, blogs, and quibs from people who wished Trump had died (sometimes miserably and painfully) or how they wouldn't have missed or how Trump deserved to die, etc. There were many government workers and regular people who ended up getting fired from their jobs over posts they wrote about killing Trump.

This whole assassination attempt by Thomas Matthew Crooks was weird because he was not made into a villain. The gun advocates didn't jump on the fact that he used an AR style rifle and demand stricter gun laws. There was no talk about focusing more on mental health; no. The focus was mostly on the sadness of many people that Crooks missed.

COVID already brought out a lot of weirdness in our culture, but Crooks brought out even more. Our culture is unique and we show it everyday. To me, it's all equally fascinating and surprising.

Table of Contents

<u>Letter To The Shooter</u>

Poetry About Thomas Matthew Crooks

1.

Address Information

Letter To The Shooter

Dear Crooks,

Butler, PA
I couldn't point it out on a map

Now, I've read
Everything I can
About your hometown
High school and
Lethal rooftop
Country fair Day

Dear Crooks,

But you ~~lived~~

GOT BULLIED

In Bethel Park –

Outside Pittsburgh:

Home of

The Deer Hunter

Put an empty chamber

In that gun!

You didn't

Dear Crooks,

Thomas Matthew Crooks

To many Trump haters

You are the crook who stole

Their hope of Trump dying

Thomas Matthew Crooks

You said you be back

At work at the nursing home

Dear Crooks,

"July 13 will be my premiere."

You wrote on Steam

But you haven't used

Discord in awhile

Your premiere has

Turned into an answerless

Rabbit hole

Dear Crooks,

Everyone around

Bethel Park claims

To know you –

Know about you

But intention

Reason

Motive and

Plan are unknown

To the point of

Pain and hurt to

Those close to

You

Dear Crooks,

The Trump Train

Never stopped

It can't stop

Not with that inner

Force pushing

And *choo choo*

Rolling rolling

Through the Steel City

And on

Dear Crooks,

Buffalo Township

Volunteer Fire

Department chief

Corey Comperatore

…also live(d) nearby

His tombstone will

Hold flowers and tears

From here on

Dear Crooks,

You wore hunting

Outfits to school often

You can't hide from the

Scrutinous eye of the teenager

Or the selfishness of the bully

A true loner is not even

Friends with his digital footprint

Fame doesn't always bring acceptance

Camo can hide you from wildlife

But society will paint you

As they want and will do so

You are now data

For the FBI for future crimes

2.

Salutation

Letter To The Shooter

Dear Crooks,

Dear ~~Hero~~

~~Bitch~~

~~Mr. Crooks~~

…What's the best way?

Dear Crooks,

Thomas, you don't know

Me. Of course, you don't

I've never been to PA

And I'd have to Google

The spelling

I live in the desert

Out west

You sure made me

Cripplingly angry

But only about humanity

Along with strong

Downhearted worry

Dear Crooks,

You searched

'Major depressive disorder'

I done similar

I used Bing, not Google,

To get detailed answers

About suicide and death

You didn't hope for and end

But an end was quickly

Thrust at you

Depression is abysmally deep

So much so that the light

Of the future is still dark –

Sometimes stygian

Dear Crooks,

You are a registered Republican

But you gave 15$ to Act Blue in 2021

You laid down on the roof

But too many have jumped –

Jumped to conclusions

Jumped to comfort

In confirmation bias

Your lack of writings left

About politics have been fuel

For fanfiction and meanderings

All around

Amid this election cycle

Circling pure anger

Dear Crooks,

You worked at a

Nursing home

You worked around

Death

An empty room

An empty bed

Is not from a checkout

Or someone going home

Some families never visit

Leaving their relatives

Lonely – loners

Not by choice, like you

Dear Crooks,

You were rejected

From your high school's

Rifle Team

Rejected by those who

Could have become friends

How can we create A.I.

But bullying is still

Everywhere – a

Solution elusive?

You were pushed into

Corners so much

You climbed to the roof

For space to breathe

Dear Crooks,

I don't wish the death on anyone

And I don't agree with murder

(except, maybe, Gary Plauché)

Because of differing political stances

(Marvin Heemeyer's killdozer

destruction is an exception)

Okay okay I am no better than

Those I judged for wishing

Trump had died on July 13th

Letter To The Shooter

3.

Body

Letter To The Shooter

Dear Crooks,

You are the one Zoomer

With a little digital footprint

People want a reason

They wait with bated breath

I, too, hope for a manifesto pdf

Words you typed in hopes

Of silencing the bullies

And finding some meaning

Your smartphone data

Is telling us some

As my poetry only repeats

The repetitious headlines

Dear Media,

Why do we know

So much about

Luigi Mangione

And so little about

Thomas Matthew Crooks?

I know you think

We are all morons,

But we know

Dear Crooks,

You bought a five foot ladder

And fifty rounds of ammunition

To use with the AR style rifle you

Borrowed from your father

To what end?

You brought suspicion

From others and police

You shot from too long away

Memes were quickly made

From photos of your bloody corpse

Giving you that digital footprint

You didn't have

Social media posts wishing Trump

Had died – some hoping for a more

Vicious death

With no creativity

They brought up cliched

Comparisons linking Trump

To Hitler

Dear Crooks,

You shot

And many on social media

Shot their shot –

Breaking United States

Code Title 18, Section 871

Many lost their jobs –

Fired and let go

Even Tenacious D

Stopped creating

Because Kyle shot

His shot for a joke

That fell like a

Bullet casing

Dear Crooks,

If it was Biden

(I know)

Who got the earshot

The Republican reaction

Would have been the same

(I know)

They would have wished

For Biden's death

And lamented the poor shot

(I know)

The Democrats don't have

A monopoly on their

Illegal hatred

Dear Crooks,

You researched

Ethan Crumbly

Your idol, apparently

The crumb that you

Pinched and grabbed

You wanted more

You planned something

I should write him

In prison

Will he answer?

Dear Crooks,

Shouldn't Qanon

Have predicted this?

That was a rhetorical

Question for you

You are not part

Of prophecy

Dear Crooks,

Did you pick Trump

Because of proximity

To your house?

If anyone from

The Royal Family

Had blessed

Bethel Farms

Or if Biden had

Given a speech

There first, we –

We would be

Betwixt a different

Social media rhetoric

LETTER FROM A TRUMP HATER

The nomination hadn't happened yet

No VP had been chosen yet

Many among the Republicans

Were worried about Trump

You missed by such a short distance

So minimal – almost microscopic

The lying and the hate could have

Stopped

No more giving a voice to hate

Elsewhere

I don't care it it's illegal

I wish Trump was dead

Rallying that kind of hate

Is horrible for our country

We had to suffer enough

When he was president

Not again – not again

Who else would the

Republicans run?

Biden would've surely

Won and you would have

Been a hero

But you missed?

It wasn't that far

It would have been

Like shooting Hitler

I dream of you

NOT missing

The Nazis need their

Leader to die

So they can lose

Their way

Letter To The Shooter

F*** them

F*** Trump

LETTER FROM A TRUMP SUPPORTER

Where's my box of bandages?

I need to show support

I will wear one everyday

You have given us

Our martyr

Only by the Grace of

God in Heaven was

Trump saved

He's the only one

Who can clear the swamp

And bring our country

Back to greatness

You are dead

And in Hell right now

Burning and suffering –

Where you should be

Trump is now the

Republican nominee

And will be 47

Definitely

LETTER FROM ME

I was angry

My optimism in humanity

Was chinked

Like knight's armor

I saw the death wishes

From those who claimed

They valued life but

Trump didn't

LETTER TO FRANCISCO MARTIN DURAN

I shall write him again

I did many months back

He tried to assassinate

Bill Clinton when he

Was president

He said he regretted everything

And was in a bad place

Mentally at that time

I am curious

Naturally so

I need to know

And since because

Of you

My world was blown

I need to know more

Dear Crooks,

Your bike is

Still there

Under the tree

In the shade

Everything

Depends on the

Lonely bike

Dear Crooks,

At 5:52 pm

You were

Spotted

And left

There

Not even the

Rolling winds

Through fresh cut

Lawns and

Happy neighbors

Kept you away

On that

Fateful day

At 5:52 pm

Letter To The Shooter

4.

Valediction

Dear Crooks,

You took his ear, dude –

Or, part of it

It's quite ironic, really

Since Trump

Hardly ever listens

Dear Crooks,

Mike Tyson, at least,

Bit Holyfield's ear off

Like a real aggressor

Dear Crooks,

Butler County Sheriff

Michael T. Slupe

Saw you and

Followed

He stared down

The barrel of your

Gun and dropped down

Before you were dropped

This is an afterthought

Overshadowed by

Other things unknown

Dear Crooks,

Slupe's name should,

However, be remembered

Along with Coperatore RIP

We need to

Watch David Dutch

And James Copernhaver

Closely as the heal

Dear Crooks,

A quarter of an inch

From hitting his head

Most people

Can't read a tape measure

But we all know that

Distance is very very

Small

To a sniper, however,

That distance is

Great

Dear Crooks,

Pop

Ear

Pop

Pop

(or was it five?)

Down

Fist raised

Dear Crooks,

You created a trend

The ear bandage

Letter To The Shooter

5.

Post-Script

Letter To The Shooter

Dear Crooks,

"I said to myself, 'Wow, what was that?
It can only be a bullet.' And moved my
right hand to my ear, brought it down.
My hand was covered with blood."

Those were Trump's

Actual words

You never got to

Hear

Dear Crooks,

When doing your

Drone surveillance

Did you not stand

In awe over the tech

And view of the

Greenery and farm

Grounds?

Dear Crooks,

CHEESE AUCTION – WEDNESDAY, AUGUST 7, AT 8:00 PM in the Dairy Pavilion. CHOICE CHEESE FROM CONTENTED COWS!

This is something worth

Waiting for

Everyone loves Cheese

You just needed to

Wait a few weeks

Dear Crooks,

Priority Crane Rentals

Needs their

Two cranes back

Black Diamond

Equipment Rentals

Needs their

Six pieces of

Equipment back, too

The rippling effect of your

Gunfire has expanded

Further than our

Societal apathy

Dear Crooks,

We are grieved by the tragic event that occurred at the Butler Farm Show grounds during former President Donald J. Trump's rally on Saturday, July 13. Our thoughts and condolences are with the family and friends of Corey Comperatore, whose life made a profound impact within the Butler community. We also extend our heartfelt sympathies to those who were injured during the incident and wish them a full recovery.

Their letter was nice

This was the beginning –

Which is what we all

Need sometimes

Just a small step or

Even one toe sliding

Forward in the sand

Dear Crooks,

Conspiracy theories

Flew around like

Drunken eagles

On July 13th

Of course, America

We did like that

But those ideas

Were clouded by

The death wishes

Dear Crooks,

P.S. We can all do better

I'm no better than anyone else

I was hypocritical during

These deathless days

6.

Walking to the Mailbox

Letter To The Shooter

Dear Crooks,

This is not a hagiography

About Trump

This is not a hagiography

About Crooks

I'm not MAGA

I'm not a serial killer fangirl

Dear Crooks,

Emails are common nowadays

Handwritten letters are special

But, many youth don't know

The structure of a letter

Or how to even address

And envelope and where

To put the stamp

Generations have changed

Have Gen X and the

Millennials made life

Easier for you Zoomers?

Dear Crooks,

The blue mailbox

Standing there

With flyers and

Gross all over it

A little graffiti

Here and there

By the time

The letter would

Get to you

(if you were

in prison)

We would be

On to something

Else – the hacking

That crashed all the

Computers and

Biden dropping out

Of the presidential race

And our slacktivism

Will rule like a

Kakistocracy

Dear Crooks,

Your momma

Gonna miss you

Dear Crooks,

I can't send you anything

But I wrote an open letter

For you, who turned my

World around and askew

Letter To The Shooter

www.ingramcontent.com/pod-product-compliance
Lightning Source LLC
Chambersburg PA
CBHW020342290526
45785CB00005B/2145